FindingGod

Our response to God's gifts

Finding God

Our response to God's gifts

Serving the Catechetical Mission
of the Church

James P. Campbell

LOYOLAPRESS.

CHICAGO

LOYOLAPRESS.

Loyola Press is an apostolate of the Chicago Province of the Society of Jesus. We embrace the Jesuit passion for helping people of all ages to find God in all things. In the sixteenth century, the visionary yet always practical St. Ignatius Loyola reminded the Jesuit theologians advising bishops at the Council of Trent to also spend time in the city streets teaching the Catholic faith to children.

In the twenty-first century, *Finding God: Our Response to God's Gifts* is born from that same Ignatian desire to help everyone discover God's love and care for them. Children and their parents are the immediate focus of this program, consciously designed as a foundation for total parish catechesis.

Serving the Catechetical Mission of the Church summarizes the history of the Church's catechetical ministry since the time of Jesus. In doing so it establishes a context for understanding how *Finding God: Our Response to God's Gifts* draws on the wisdom of the Catholic tradition to meet the challenges of today.

George A. Lane, S.J.
Publisher

Introduction

Finding God: Our Response to God's Gifts reflects the wisdom catechists have acquired in more than two thousand years of the Church's history about sharing the message of who Jesus Christ is and how he is calling us in the Holy Spirit to God our Father.

In these two thousand years, languages, technologies, and social circumstances have changed. The Church was conceived in the political and social environment of the Jewish-Palestinian world. The Romans controlled Palestine, as they did all the lands surrounding the Mediterranean Sea. The early apostles and disciples went first to the synagogues in the ancient Near East to proclaim the coming of the Messiah. The writings of the New Testament reflect the struggles of the early Church and the hostility that existed between the believers in Jesus and those who rejected the message of the disciples.

In the year A.D. 67, a Jewish rebellion brought the Roman army into Palestine, crushing any resistance in the countryside. Jerusalem fell when the Romans broke through the walls, plundered the city, and destroyed the temple. In the decades following the destruction of the Temple, Judaism began to redefine itself as a religion of the book rather than as a religion of sacrifice.

In these same decades, the early Christian Church experienced a transition as well. Following the example of Paul, the early Church moved from the Jewish-Christian environment into that of the Greco-Roman world. In the next three hundred years as the Christian Church grew, it existed on the margins of a society suspicious of its values. Therefore the process of the Catechumenate was developed to initiate believers into Christian life. The development of this new process was the first of many transitions for the Church. As languages, technologies, and social circumstances have changed, the Church has created or adapted strategies to address the people's need to hear the gospel of hope in Jesus Christ.

With the fall of the Roman Empire in the West, bishops and monks of the Church established stable institutions that provided a foundation for medieval civilization. In catechesis the memory of Jesus was kept alive in the memorization of the Apostles' Creed and the Lord's Prayer. Catholic shrines celebrating the lives of the saints and their willingness to intercede for the needy provided the people with an accessible spirituality that gave them hope.

During medieval times Christians in Western Europe were immersed in a culture of Christian images and vocabulary. But the Mass continued to be celebrated in Latin and became less relevant in people's devotional life. As the Church moved into the sixteenth century, religious and social limitations created the conditions that led to the Reformation and to divisions within Christendom.

Saint Ignatius of Loyola ministered to the Church in the midst of this turmoil. He realized that the great need for the Church was the "care of souls," and in the *Spiritual Exercises* he developed a method that would help people grow in a personal relationship with Jesus and with the Church in service to the world.

The situation of the Church today is not unlike that which faced Ignatius. We are in the middle of a communications and social revolution. Believers need coherent methods that will help them learn and communicate the Christian faith. They need articulate models that can be used to pass on Catholic teaching. They need prayer strategies that will help them grow in a personal relationship with God and others.

Finding God: Our Response to God's Gifts is formed upon the *Catechism of the Catholic Church*, the *General Directory for Catechesis*, and other significant documents on catechesis. It was also created to reflect the principles of personal and spiritual development that are basic to Ignatian spirituality. We believe that this powerful combination of teaching and methodology makes a positive contribution to meet the ever-shifting challenges of the contemporary world. Chapters 3–10 give a historical sketch of how the Church has adapted catechetical strategies to meet the needs of changing social situations. Chapter 11 reflects on the catechetical documents that are the intellectual foundation of the program. Finally chapters 12–15 explore Ignatius of Loyola's own passion for sharing the faith and discuss in detail how the Ignatian spirituality is infused in the program.

CHAPTER 1

Religious Education in the Time of Jesus

Religious education in the time of Jesus was rooted in the Scriptures, in what we presently call the Old Testament. Religious instruction introduced the Jewish people into a way of life based on laws of conduct toward God and their neighbor as found in the Torah, the first five books of the Old Testament. This was the "teaching" or the "Law."

The Purpose of Religious Education

Two overarching purposes shaped religious education in the Jewish community. First, the people were to learn their own history, which was the story of their relationship to God through God's covenant with them. Second, the people were to build their lives upon the ideals and values set forth in the Scriptures.

Through storytelling and religious celebrations, the people learned about the redemption of their ancestors from slavery in Egypt, their wanderings after the Exodus, and their entrance into the Promised Land. They learned how the Ten Commandments were given on Mount Sinai and how these commandments were to guide their lives in faithfulness to God as practiced in compassionate concern for one another. They learned about those who lived in faithfulness to God, especially Moses, Joshua, and King David. This history also provided examples of individuals and communities who did not follow God. When they made sinful choices, turning against God and one another, they had to face the consequences of their choices.

Called to Be Holy

Through the teachings of the Old Testament scriptures, God called the people to live holy lives, worshiping God alone and treating one another with reverence. Aging parents were to be cared for. The poor were seen as special in God's eyes, and the people were to let the poor and strangers gather the grain left in their fields after the harvest. The people were prohibited from stealing from one another or dealing with one another dishonestly. Any actions that oppressed neighbors, servants, or those who were physically handicapped were forbidden. Social relationships were to be modeled on God's justice. God demonstrated his justice by giving his people freedom. The people were to emulate God's justice by doing what they could to liberate one another. God's justice was reflected in his concern for the poor and the outcast, and, in turn, the people were to show concern for others through individual and community action.

Holiness in the life of a Jew was based upon the holiness of God. Living out God's values required first of all a healthy "fear of the Lord." When the people remembered all that God had done for them, they accepted their responsibility to act toward one another as God had acted toward them.

Responsibility of Parents

Parents, especially the father, were responsible for the religious formation of the family. The father told the stories of the Exodus and the receiving of the Ten Commandments. The father would especially teach the *Shema,* the prayer from Deuteronomy 6: 4–9 that was said every morning and every evening.

> Hear, O Israel! The LORD is our God, the LORD alone! Therefore, you shall love the LORD, your God, with all your heart, and with all your soul, and with all your strength. Take to heart these words which I enjoin on you today. Drill them into your children. Speak of them at home and abroad, whether you are busy or at rest. Bind them at your wrist as a sign and let them be as a pendant on your forehead. Write them on the doorposts of your houses and on your gates.

The ideals of Jewish religious education were also articulated in the first seven verses of Psalm 78

Attend, my people, to my teaching;
　listen to the words of my mouth.
I will open my mouth in story,
　drawing lessons from of old.
We have heard them, we know them;
　our ancestors have recited them to us.
We do not keep them from our children;
　we recite them to the next generation,
The praiseworthy and mighty deeds of the LORD,
　the wonders that he performed.
God set up a decree in Jacob,
　established a law in Israel:
What he commanded our ancestors,
　they were to teach their children;
That the next generation might come to know,
　children yet to be born.
In turn they were to recite them to their children,
　that they too might put their trust in God,
And not forget the works of God,
　keeping his commandments.

How Jesus Learned

Education in the time of Jesus was primarily religious. God was at the center of all life and culture. For the Jews, all truth came from God. Truth was not an abstract discussion about what was or was not factual. The person who lived in truth was someone who trusted God's teaching to lead to health and happiness. God was creator, judge, and redeemer of the people and the one who knew what was best for all. Every day in the life of a faithful Jew was a day of prayer.

In his book *Christology: True God, True Man*, Matthias Neuman, O.S.B. comments,

It may come as a surprise to learn that the primary setting in which Jesus would have prayer was his daily routine of life and work. The prayer that most marked the pious Jew was (and is) the praying of the *Shema*, that fundamental expression of Jewish faith. . . . It was the responsibility of the

3

observant Jew to pray at least three times a day—morning, late afternoon, and evening—wherever he was (home, marketplace, field) and whatever one was doing (working, relaxing, spending time with friends), the *Shema* called to mind and expressed the reality of Israel's God and the relationship between God and Israel, and between God and the individual believer.[1]

Temple and Synagogue

When Jesus was growing up, the central place of Jewish prayer and learning was the temple in Jerusalem. The importance of the temple in Jesus' life is reflected in the Gospels, especially the stories of the boy Jesus with the religious scholars (Luke 2:41–52), and the record of Jesus' actions banishing the money lenders from the temple precincts (John 2:13–22).

While the temple was important for the major feasts and sacrifices, the local synagogue was the center of activity for individual communities. In the synagogues they gathered to pray and to hear the Scriptures read. The institution of the synagogue began to develop between 587 B.C. and 537 B.C., when many Jews were exiled from Jerusalem and settled in Babylon (present-day Iraq). The synagogue became a place of assembly where all the concerns of Jewish life could be discussed. People came to pray, worship, and learn.

According to the Gospel of Luke, Jesus began his ministry in Galilee, meeting with community leaders in a synagogue. Reading from the scroll of Isaiah, Jesus proclaimed,

> "The Spirit of the Lord is upon me,
> because he has anointed me
>   to bring glad tidings to the poor.
> He has sent me to proclaim liberty to captives
>   and recovery of sight to the blind,
>   to let the oppressed go free,
> and to proclaim a year acceptable to the Lord."

Rolling up the scroll, he handed it back to the attendant and sat down, and the eyes of all in the synagogue looked intently at him. He said to them, "Today this scripture passage is fulfilled in your hearing." (Luke 4:18–21)

The Destruction of the Temple and the Synagogue

The temple in Jerusalem ceased to be the center of Jewish spiritual life after the year A.D. 70. In A.D. 68, the Jews had risen in political revolt against the Roman Empire. Rome brought in its massive, efficient armies to crush the rebellion. The Romans lay siege to Jerusalem, eventually coming over the walls to destroy the city and the temple.

With the destruction of the temple, the synagogue became the most important gathering place for Jews. The Jewish people had to refocus their religious life. Because the animal sacrifices (as spelled out in Leviticus and elsewhere) could take place only in the temple, they now disappeared from Jewish religious practice. Those Jews who survived the disastrous fall of the temple refocused their energies on gathering in the synagogues and commenting upon the Scriptures (Old Testament). For example, Jewish religious leaders decided that only those Old Testament books that were written in Hebrew could be considered inspired by God. Commentary on the Scriptures and the interpretation of their meaning became an important discipline for Jewish life. The faithful Jew now concentrated on making every day holy and acceptable to God. Every action was to be dedicated to God.

The synagogues were also important to the Jewish people as they emigrated throughout the Mediterranean world to settle in cities such as Alexandria in Egypt, Athens in Greece, and Rome. Jews in these strange lands could gather in synagogues for community support and prayer. When the early apostles and disciples traveled through the known world to preach faith in Jesus, they began by speaking in synagogues, because people in those communities already knew the Scriptures and could therefore identify Jesus as the Messiah.

Thus from the Jews' earliest days, religious education was paramount to their existence as a people. This was the environment in which Jesus grew up and learned. With the destruction of the temple and the resulting loss of a tribal center, the Scriptures gained even more importance in individual communities. And community itself remained a life-giving force for Jews no matter where they lived.

CHAPTER 2

Jesus as Teacher

Jesus' disciples experienced him first as a teacher. Throughout the New Testament, Jesus is most often identified by the terms *teacher* or *rabbi,* which are used some sixty-five times. Jesus taught publicly in the countryside, in local synagogues, and in the temple at Jerusalem. He also taught his disciples privately as he prepared them for their mission. It was common practice at that time for a rabbi to gather students and indoctrinate them with his particular teaching of Scriptures, thus establishing his own school of interpretation. Although Jesus did interpret Scriptures, opening up their meaning according to his own role as Messiah, he did not focus upon building a school of thought. Jesus' foremost teaching was that he was the one who understood God's true relationship with people. Jesus sent his disciples to teach that he was the one especially sent by God.

Jesus taught in the form of parables. Vivid stories and examples gave the listener a new insight into God and into how God wanted people to relate to others. People who took his parables to heart realized that if they were to serve the kingdom Jesus proclaimed they had to make a radical choice.

Proclaiming the Kingdom of God

Jesus proclaimed the imminent coming of the kingdom of God. He urged his followers to repent and believe the gospel. He compared the proclamation of the kingdom to that of a seed sown in a field. From the smallest seed, a bush could grow that would be large enough for birds to nest in (Matthew 13:31–32). In like manner, from those few people who first received Jesus' word in faith, God's kingdom would grow.

Jesus taught that the kingdom was to be proclaimed especially to the poor and lowly. He was sent to "preach the good news to the poor," whom the Father had proclaimed blessed. Jesus shared his own life with the poor. He experienced the hunger, privation, and thirst that the poor experienced every day. Jesus made active concern for the poor a prerequisite for anyone who wished to enter his kingdom.

The story of Jesus and the rich young man is a good example of the kind of choice he was calling people to make (Mark 10:17–31). The rich young man was a faith-filled person. He followed the commandments, honored his parents, and cared for others. He asked Jesus if this was enough. Jesus challenged the young man to go a step further—to sell what he had, give it to the poor, and follow Jesus. This upset the young man, because his riches were very important to him. Jesus was suggesting that he turn away from his material goods and the lifestyle they supported. The Gospel of Luke tells us that Jesus was saddened as the young man walked away (Luke 18:24). The young man was walking away from a life of discipleship, a transformation of life that could enable him to make a deeper commitment to God and others.

Inviting the Sinner

Jesus made a point to invite "sinners" into the kingdom. At that time in Palestine, anyone who did not, or could not, live within the requirements of Old Testament law was considered a sinner. Such a person could be shunned by other Jews as unworthy of being a child of God. Jesus invited sinners to be in relationship with him and assured them of God's love for them. God's love and mercy was not contained within a system of laws but was boundless. Jesus illustrated God's care and concern in the story of the lost sheep, emphasizing the joy in heaven when one sinner repented.

Jesus' teaching and call to discipleship angered many people who heard him. His message was so disturbing that religious and political leaders plotted to kill him. And so Jesus was arrested, tried, and crucified. To an unknowing world, it was merely the execution of a criminal. Jesus' disciples, however, saw these events through the eyes of faith, and they recognized that the God who became man sacrificed himself so our sins could be forgiven.

CHAPTER 3

Jesus Christ Is Proclaimed: Catechesis in the Early Church

The story in Luke 24:13–35 about the two disciples on the road to Emmaus illustrates the transformation that the disciples in the early Church experienced after Jesus' crucifixion. The disciples moved from despondent followers who had witnessed the death of Jesus to hopeful believers who met him as the risen Lord. At first they did not recognize the stranger on the road who instructed them on the meaning of Jesus' life and death. Encouraged by their conversation, they reached out to share bread with him. But when Jesus broke the bread, the disciples discovered to their inexpressible delight that the stranger was none other than the risen Jesus Christ.

The Risen Jesus Christ Proclaimed

After forty days, during which he appeared to many of his disciples, Jesus ascended into heaven while standing in their midst. Then, again, after some time had passed, the Holy Spirit came to Jesus' apostles and disciples, helping them to recognize the deeper implications of Jesus' resurrection and ascension. Under the influence of the Holy Spirit they recognized Jesus Christ as the Lord, who now sat at the right hand of God the Father. With their savior now with the Father, they appreciated even more the prayer he had taught them, recognizing the Lord's Prayer as the most important prayer for them to learn and to teach. They also realized that the Holy Spirit was calling them to become the Church. As the Church and body of Christ, they proclaimed the meaning of Jesus' life, death, resurrection, and ascension, calling all people to salvation..

Jesus' apostles and disciples proclaimed his gospel first in the synagogues, sharing with their Jewish community of faith the message that the Messiah had come in Jesus Christ. Eventually they followed the example of Paul and went to the Gentiles, proclaiming that the Son of God had come to earth to save all and to call all people into the Kingdom of God.

Early Catechetical Methods

The gospel of Jesus Christ was first proclaimed in stories. Having few books to read from, early disciples acted out the stories so they could vividly communicate the dramatic impact of the events they were describing. Poetic memory techniques such as those that we find in the Beatitudes (Matthew 5:1–10) helped the people to remember the concepts more easily. The parables that Jesus taught the disciples they now repeated to others, giving listeners vivid images to help them relate to God as loving Father. As they listened to the stories and witnessed the faith of the early Church, people— some Jews and some not—were moved to accept the grace of the Holy Spirit to become Christians. The sincerity of the early disciples spoke with the people heart-to-heart. As the apostle Paul states in Romans 10:14–15, 17

> But how can they call on him in whom they have not believed? And how can they believe in him of whom they have not heard? And how can they hear without someone to preach? And how can people preach unless they are sent? As it is written, "How beautiful are the feet of those who bring [the] good news!" Thus faith comes from what is heard, and what is heard comes through the word of Christ.

The Early Written Tradition

The teaching of the early Church began to be seen in written form with the apostle Paul's First Letter to the Thessalonians, composed about A.D. 55. As time went on, Paul would write more letters to the Romans, Galatians, Corinthians, and Philippians, and a private letter to Philemon. The sayings of Jesus and the stories about him would also be gathered and shaped into the Gospel accounts, beginning with the Gospel of Mark in about A.D. 65 through Matthew and Luke around A.D. 80 and the Gospel of John about the year A.D. 90. These, in addition to other epistles by James, John, Jude, the epistle to the Hebrews, the letters to the Colossians, Ephesians, and Timothy, and finally the book of Revelation, would comprise the New Testament.

> These writings reflect the faith of the apostolic Church, giving us vivid portraits of Jesus, and with the Old Testament form the fundamental teachings for all catechesis. The Gospels are especially important as they "are the heart of all the Scriptures 'because they are our principal source for the life and teaching of the Incarnate Word, our Savior.'" [*Dei Verbum* 18] (CCC 125)

CHAPTER 4

The World the Early Church Catechized

The early Church lived in a world hostile to Christian values. Those who wished to become Christian were introduced into a way of life based on a close relationship with Jesus Christ. They understood that this relationship could grow only in the context of the life of the Church. In accepting Christ, they also accepted the mission of the Church to proclaim the gospel and lead others to life in Christ.

The Christian Church spread from Palestine into the Mediterranean world, which was controlled by the Romans and reflected the ideals of Greek civilization. It was a world of highly literate and sophisticated city-states. It was also a multicultural world expressing many differing religious beliefs. The Romans were ready to respect local religious beliefs as long as worship of the Roman Emperor as a god could be folded into the mix. The Roman rulers were interested primarily in collecting taxes, not orchestrating belief systems.

Thus the Roman authorities recognized the Jewish religion. But the early Christian Church was not accepted as a tolerated religious entity. When Christians met to pray, the Romans saw them as an illegal assembly. So right away the Christian Church was vulnerable to persecution. In the first centuries of the Church's existence, persecutions were local affairs. Nero's famous persecution in about A.D. 64 was limited to the city of Rome. There was no Empire wide persecution until the reign of Decius (A.D. 249–251).

Systematic persecution continued sporadically through the reign of the Emperor Diocletian (284–305) until A.D. 312. While not always actively persecuted, Christians usually kept a low profile. In order to protect themselves and to assess the sincerity of potential converts, they created a lengthy process of initiation into the church. The first step in this time of preparation was the catechumenate.

The Catechumenate

When someone wanted to become a Christian, he or she needed to have a Christian sponsor who would speak for the initiate's good will. The sponsor introduced the initiate and mentored that person through a time of discernment and prayer called the catechumenate. The bishop, who was normally the pastor of the local church, was responsible for catechesis. Catechumens were not introduced into the full Christian life until they were well advanced in the process. For instance, they did not learn the Lord's Prayer until late in the initiation process because in the view of Roman authorities it was a subversive prayer, proclaiming that God, not the Roman emperor, was the true Father. One reason this was done was to protect the community in case an insincere catechumen would report to the authorities that Christians were enemies of the state.

In the period of initiation catechumens memorized a profession of faith (the Apostles' Creed was the profession of faith for the Church in Rome) and finally participated fully in the liturgy. Each stage of the process of initiation, which could last from several months to years, demanded an ever-deepening commitment on the part of the catechumen to a transformation of heart leading up to baptism. Catechumens recognized that they were being led into a new way of life centered on Christ. Some catechumens had to make decisions to leave the army or to cease practicing immoral professions such as prostitution before they could move forward. At the end of the process, catechumens were baptized at the Easter Vigil and brought forward as full members of the Church. They deepened their commitment to Christian life through ongoing catechesis as the bishop continued to teach the Scriptures and their meaning for daily life.

The Catechumenal Model Today

The Second Vatican Council has revived the catechumenate as the principle model for catechesis in the church today. The *General Directory for Catechesis* reinforces the importance of this model.

> The model for all catechesis is the baptismal catechumenate when, by specific formation, an adult converted to belief is brought to explicit profession of baptismal faith during the Paschal Vigil. (180) This catechumenal formation should inspire the other forms of catechesis in both their objectives and in their dynamism. (*GDC* 59)

CHAPTER 5

Catechesis in the Age of Christian Empire, 300–600

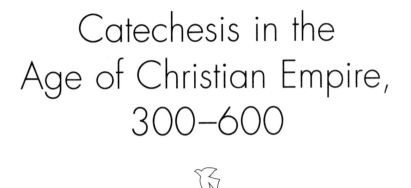

The conversion of the Roman Emperor Constantine to Christianity dramatically changed the status of the Church. Instead of living on the margins of society, the Church became the predominant source of spiritual and political influence within the Roman Empire.

The Impact of Constantine on the Christian Church

Everything changed for the church with the acceptance of Christianity by Constantine, who was emperor of the Roman Empire from 306–337. Constantine began as first a coemperor with Maxentius. This lasted until Constantine defeated Maxentius in a battle in Italy at the Milvian Bridge outside of Rome October 29, 312. Constantine attributed his victory to the One God that Christians worshiped. He also saw that the Christian faith, with its belief in one God, could support his goal to be the single emperor ruling the Roman Empire. The Christian Church would take care of the spiritual needs of the people; he, as God's vicar, would rule politically in God's name.

[Constantine] immediately began to enfranchise the Church, granting it land and property, raising the clergy to a position of honor and privilege in the empire, exempting them from municipal duties and taxes, permitting them jurisdiction over some legal matters. In all, Christianity emerged from its disfavor and became central to the civic and the religious life of the empire.[2]

The financial resources of the state now supported Christian initiatives. Bishops and priests received state salaries. Money was made available for the building of basilicas and monasteries. Many of the nobility now became Christians in great numbers, seeing the Church as a path to further their social and political advancement. While the catechumenate process continued, there was now the need to catechize many who were quickly baptized.

The Role of the Bishops

In the centuries between 300 and 600, the Roman Empire in Western Europe was in the process of disintegration, internally through moral decay and externally under the pressure of Germanic invaders. As Imperial society splintered, people turned to the Church for protection from predatory tax collectors within and from the invaders coming from beyond the borders of the Empire.

In this period of growing despair, the voice of hope was generally that of the Christian bishop. The Christian bishops were the principal catechists. This was the era of great bishops and catechists such as Ambrose, bishop of Milan (374–397), and Augustine of Hippo (354–430). They defended the poor, taught through their homilies and writings, and created the foundations of Christian doctrine. The bishops negotiated with the leaders of the invading tribes and attempted to keep them from looting and destroying the cities. In 452 Pope Saint Leo I persuaded Attila to withdraw his army of Huns from Italy. Later in 455 when the Vandals plundered Rome, Leo I was able to protect the people from murder and arson.

The teachings of these great bishops, especially those of Augustine of Hippo, provided a vocabulary for understanding how Christians should live. Their writings were copied and preserved to provide the foundation of Church teaching.

Catechesis in the Later Roman Empire

Catechesis was primarily the responsibility of the bishop. He trained and supervised the priests and deacons, who catechized the catechumens. The bishop himself would often give the concluding instructions during Lent that led up to the rites of initiation celebrated during the Easter Vigil.

Catechesis was done within the context of liturgical celebration. Catechumens were prepared for initiation, the rites were explained, and liturgical preaching took place in the midst of the assembly that gathered for worship. Christian education was primarily to adults, who heard the call of the gospel through the proclamation and exploration of the Scriptures in the context of the liturgy. This teaching they took into their hearts and home to teach their children.

In the case of children born into Christian homes, the parents were the principle catechists and sponsors in the faith. It was the bishops who had the responsibility of guiding the parents in providing religious instruction, and who set the standard both for teaching and theological reflection.

As there was no Catholic school system, children learned in the secular schools. That way they could learn Greek, the language in which the Bible was written. Catechesis consisted mainly of Bible stories that were read at home. The Sunday homily gave the bishop opportunity to comment on the stories and deepen the Christian's understanding of their meaning.

CHAPTER 6

Catechesis in a Chaotic Time, 600–1100

The date usually given for the fall of the Western Roman Empire is 476 when Romulus Augustulus, the last ruler to carry the name of emperor, was deposed. Political power diversified to local rulers. Between 533 and 540 the Eastern Roman emperor Justinian (527–565) sent his armies to reclaim the glory of Rome in North Africa and Italy. While his attempt seemed to succeed militarily, Italy was left devastated from the pillaging armies. Justinian was said to have created a desert and called it "peace."

A World Falling Apart

The period between A.D. 600 and 1000 in Western Europe has been called the Dark Ages. The brittle cosmopolitan civilization of the Roman Empire in the West had shattered under the impact of raids conducted by tribes from Northern Europe and Central Asia. For centuries the Germanic tribes had lived on the periphery of Roman civilization. As internal coherence in the Empire broke down, the tribal leaders saw an opportunity to expand; they made their entrance, settled in the fertile agricultural valleys, and raided the cities for their wealth.

Catholic bishops in the Dark Ages were increasingly thrust into political power as civil authority vanished. Bishops negotiated with the tribal leaders, organized relief for the destitute, and managed to protect enough of the social structure for civil life to survive. The Church's authority was increasingly centered on the church in Rome. The Church had the task of evangelizing the descendants of the invading tribes to Catholic Christianity as they settled in Western Europe. The Church also preserved the cultural memory of the Roman Empire and introduced these new people to an ideal of civilization.

The Role of the Monasteries

During these centuries of disorder and confusion, raiding parties of Saracens in the Mediterranean region or Vikings from the north ransacked the agricultural villages that struggled to survive from year to year. Yet the monasteries that were established throughout Europe based on the *Rule* of Saint Benedict of Nursia (A.D. 480–550) provided signs of hope. The monks cleared and cultivated the land, built churches and living quarters, and collected and copied ancient manuscripts, preserving them in libraries for later generations. Monasteries were islands of stability in a violent world. They were also seen as a source of spiritual strength as the monks prayed not only for themselves but also for the needs of the world.

The Importance of the Saints

Especially important for Christians was the work of the saints on their behalf. Shrines to patron saints, like that of Martin of Tours in southern France, were important places of pilgrimage. Stories of the valiant deeds of the saints and the many miracles attributed to them gave hope to people who were afraid of what each day might bring. The stability of Roman rule was replaced by local rulers who raided one another's lands. People were at the mercy of the armies that crossed and crisscrossed their lands.

> Frankish society was based on the might of the king and the binding ties of mutual tribal obligation. Without a strong king at its center, Frankish political life was fraught with treachery and violence, a world of feuding families and powerful patrons. In such a world, Roman Catholic bishops claimed the

supernatural patronage of their saints. These saints, like Saint Martin of Tours, acted as the Church's warrior-protectors from beyond the grave, imitating on a supernatural level the social structure of the Franks.[3]

Catechesis in Turbulent Times

During this period of social and spiritual dislocation, the catechumenate was forgotten. The social structure that supported the process of the Christian journey as one in which the catechumen spent months or years being initiated into life in Christ no longer existed. Germanic tribes were converted en masse, with whole peoples being baptized to follow the lead of their ruler. The Church now had the task of bringing postbaptismal instruction to a basically nonliterate population.

Catechesis was done mainly through preaching. Stories of the saints, about the wonders of healing and protection, were taught to show the power of the Church to overcome the world. In these troublesome times the people looked for spiritual allies who could help them in their daily lives. The shrines of the saints became places of pilgrimage, their relics signs of the divine being present in the world and ready to help. The people were taught the power of intercessory prayer, and they prayed that the saints intercede for them in their time of need.

The fundamental teaching required of all Christians was to memorize the Lord's Prayer and the Apostles' Creed. It was the responsibility of parents to teach these to their children. St. Eligius (d. c. 658, bishop of Noyen, France) stressed this responsibility.

> Know by memory the Symbol [Creed] and the Lord's Prayer, and teach them to your children. Instruct and admonish the children, whom you have received newborn from the baptismal fount, to live ever in the fear of God. Know that you have taken an oath on their behalf before God.[4]

As rudimentary as these catechetical efforts seem, they were strong enough for Christian life to survive and later flourish. The work of missionary bishops such as Saint Boniface (680–754), the political efforts of Charlemagne (742–814), and the educational efforts of the monastic communities became the foundation of a new civilization.

CHAPTER 7

The Church Builds a New Civilization, 1100–1500

From 1100 to 1500, the Church was established as the most powerful spiritual and, at times, political force in Europe. In Western Europe, trade began to grow and cities began to flourish. Increasing prosperity allowed the building of cathedrals and the establishment of universities. The Church was deeply influential in this upward movement. The first universities were schools of Canon Law to prepare clerics for church administration. Bishops and local leadership planned, funded, and administered the building of the great cathedrals.

The Medieval Church

Medieval times were also centuries of warfare, pestilence, and death. From the Crusades beginning in 1095 to the dynastic wars of the late 1400s, various armies crossed and recrossed Europe, living off of people's land and labor. In the mid-fourteenth century, the Black Death, a combination of bubonic plague and anthrax, killed one third of the population of Western Europe.

There was hardly a state of life that was not touched by the Church. Emperors and kings were crowned and anointed in religious rites. Orders of knighthood were dedicated to saints. Commercial and craft guilds chose patron saints and celebrated their feasts with parades and festivals. Pharmacies bore religious names. Inns almost always had signs of biblical origin. Hospices for weary travelers were dedicated to the Holy Spirit.

A Catechesis of Immersion

Catechesis in Western Europe during this time was a catechesis of immersion. People born into this world entered a community life that was entirely formed by the language of Christianity. All the stages of life, beginning in baptism and ending in death, were marked and celebrated in Christian ritual.

Above all, especially in the cities, life was centered on the great cathedrals. Every segment of society participated in the building of cathedrals through contributions and volunteer labor. Stained-glass windows created radiant chapels of light and gave instruction in scenes from the Bible or the lives of the saints. Holy days were celebrated with festivals and games. Passion plays recounted the story of Jesus' crucifixion and resurrection. Other religious plays recounted the story of Everyman's journey through this vale of tears to the resurrection. In 1223 St. Francis of Assisi created the Christmas crèche, combining images from the Gospels of Matthew and Luke into a seamless story that still inspires the world today.

But in this culture that was so suffused with Christian images there was little systematic catechesis. Parents were instructed in their religious duties through the confessional and had the responsibility for instructing their children in memorizing the articles of faith, the Lord's Prayer, the Hail Mary, and the Ten Commandments. Devout Christians also had the opportunity to attend liturgical celebrations, hear the Divine Office being sung in the cathedral or local church, and participate in the celebration of the Mass. The growing practice of praying the rosary gave people the opportunity to reflect on the life of Jesus and Mary in their daily lives.

The catechesis during this period suffered some unfortunate limitations. While liturgical plays helped people to participate more fully in the Christian story, they were also filled with anti-Semitic images and teachings that promoted hateful attitudes against Jews. Some of these images remained part of the Christian liturgy until the 1960s.

Influence of Scholasticism

Still, this time of new civilization was a period of great learning. Scholars such as Saint Thomas Aquinas (1225–1274) and Saint Bonaventure (1217–1274) influenced the development of logical thought. Catholic theology was now organized according to the logical scheme promoted by Scholasticism and was presented analytically. This became the predominant scheme by which priests were taught. Priests followed this pattern of logical thinking in the preaching of their sermons, which was now the principal source of catechetical instruction to the laity.

> The "scholastic method" was a staged process of reflection and organization of thought upon theology. It first step was *lectio,* careful reading, usually of the Scriptures, with attention to details of grammar and meaning of words. This was followed by *quaestio,* or "question," inquiring into specific problems that arise out of one's reading and bringing philosophy and theology to bear upon them. After this came *disputatio,* engaging in critical conversation with fellow scholars over the argument set out in the question. Then the process culminated in the *summa,* the summary or synthesis of the results in the process of a rational and coherent order. But the last stage was always *praedicatio,* preaching and teaching with clarity and precision. So, despite its often detailed and seemingly obscure turns of phrase, scholasticism always had a practical end in mind.[5]

Under the influence of the Scholastic method, Catholic theology moved away from an emphasis on the dynamic story of salvation history beginning in the Old Testament, finding its fulfillment in the New Testament, and moving to the work of the Holy Spirit in time. Religious instruction became a process of logical thought.

The Impact of the Continuing Latin Liturgy

In the medieval Church, the liturgy was celebrated in Latin while the language of the people was developing into the mix of languages that exist in Europe today. The celebration of the Mass for the laity became a spectacle that they witnessed but did not actively participate in. One consequence was that the devotional life of the people moved away from the eucharistic center of Christian life to an even greater reliance on practicing devotions to saints and relics.

> [M]any people slipped into almost magical views of salvation, believing, for example, that people could buy or ensure their salvation through the purchase of indulgences or the performance of popular religious practices. Such confused notions, and others like them, became the avalanche of factors that contributed to the Protestant Reformation (1517–1563).[6]

Catechesis in the Reformation and Enlightenment Period, 1500–1900

We are so accustomed to printed catechetical materials that we are unaware of how revolutionary a development they were. The invention of movable-type printing by Johannes Gutenberg in 1453 led to the first printed Bibles as well as the opportunity for scholars to compare texts. The printing made it possible for Martin Luther to create the first catechism explaining Christian beliefs from Luther's perspective, and for Catholic authors such as Peter Canisius and Robert Bellarmine to create catechisms to explain and defend the Catholic faith. Printing also made possible the widespread distribution of and, subsequently, a long period of influence for the *Catechism of the Council of Trent* (also known as the *Roman Catechism*) that summarized and explained the teachings of the Council of Trent (1545–1563) and became the source for local catechisms written in Europe and the United States

Pre-Reformation History

As stated in previous chapters, in the medieval Church there were a multitude of images, sacramental events, liturgical plays, and seasons of feasts and celebrations that followed a person's spiritual life from cradle to grave. But many people began to question these practices. The mid-1300s saw the ravages of the Black Death, in which 25 to 30 percent of the European population died. While the Church was immensely powerful and influential, people began to believe that it was in need of renewal. The years 1378–1417 saw the Church in schism, with one pope in Rome and another in Avignon, France, and the whole of Christendom confused as to which one spoke with Christ's authority. The later 1400s witnessed bishops meeting in council in dispute with the pope over issues of papal authority. Into the 1500s, many in the Church recognized the need for reform.

The changes that were taking place in European society between the end of the 1400s and the beginning of the 1500s were not unlike many changes that are taking place today.

The late 1400s were years of discovery. Caravels from Portugal had rounded the southern tip of Africa and established immensely profitable trade routes to India and South Asia. Christopher Columbus, seeking a direct route to Asia, ran into North and South America. The people of Western Europe were conscious that the world was larger than they could possibly have imagined. The wealth seemed to be limitless.

Information began to flow more freely. Johannes Gutenberg's invention of movable-type printing in 1455 began to have enormous effect in the early 1500s. The printing press made possible the publication of relatively inexpensive editions of the Bible. It also made possible almost instant communication of the teachings of the reformers and the rebuttals that came from Catholic apologists.

The printing press made possible the growth of an urban literate population. It also allowed for the printing of tracts, books, and editions of the Bible from many manuscript traditions. It made possible the growth in numbers of private readers and changed the way people were taught, with the printed word becoming the authority over and against the verbal wisdom of previous generations.

These events and others caused the increasingly urban and literate population to question the social ties that had been taken for granted for more than a thousand years. Access to the printed word and the practice of solitary reading resulted in the old ties of family, tribe, and the sense of corporate identity with the Church becoming more tenuous. People began to ask the question "What must I do to be saved?" This was the question most predominant in Martin Luther's mind as a young preacher and scholar; it drove him in his studies and meditations and led to his great breakthrough in understanding and faith.

Beginning of the Reformation

In 1517 Pope Leo X allowed Margrave Albrecht of Brandenburg to combine the archdioceses of Mainz and Magdeburg under his jurisdiction. In order to do this, Albrecht had to send a large fee to Rome. Albrecht raised the money by borrowing it from the Fugger family, who were major financiers in early modern times. In order to help Albrecht service the debt he incurred, Leo X allowed him to send a preacher throughout the archdiocese to preach about the value of receiving indulgences. When the preacher, Johann Tetzel, preached about indulgences he made extravagant promises about the efficacy of prayer for releasing souls from purgatory. A donation of money would facilitate this transaction. As proof of their concern, people making the donation would receive a printed certificate of contribution. Thousands of copies of indulgence certificates were printed up and given to people as assurance that their loved ones would spring from purgatory to heaven.

This blatant commercial exploitation of the indulgence system sparked the concern of Martin Luther. He addressed his concerns by nailing a copy of his Ninety-five Theses on Indulgences on the church door in Wittenberg. It was Luther's intent to begin a local debate. Thousands of copies were printed and distributed over Northern Europe. People discovered that Luther was not alone in his concerns, and the Reformation that would shake the Church to its foundations was under way.

The Impact of Luther's Challenge

Martin Luther experienced the spiritual crisis of his time as a personal crisis of faith. As an Augustinian friar he practiced an exemplary life and diligently followed the penitential disciplines of his community. He was quite concerned about whether his sins were forgiven, and he spent many hours in confession trying to remember and tell all of his sins so he could receive absolution. He was never conscious of experiencing God's forgiveness, and he increased his penances to try to root out what he thought was the deep sinfulness in his life.

To illustrate how he saw his relationship with God, Luther told the story of himself as a young boy in the street of his hometown. Once while at play, Martin and his friends saw the butcher running toward them, arms filled with sausages. The children were frightened and ran away. Later he found out that the butcher was running to give them the sausages. For Luther this was an example of how God wants to deal with us, running toward us with love, and our constant inclination is to run away.

Luther was a Scripture scholar who was responsible for teaching the Bible to his Augustinian community. As he prepared lectures on the Psalms, and especially on Paul's Epistle to the Romans, Luther had the insight that salvation is not based on human work or effort, but is rather a new relationship with God of absolute trust in the divine promise for salvation won for us in Jesus Christ. Jesus Christ freed us from our sins and brings us salvation. The redeemed person, rather than having to work for salvation, while still a sinner is freely and fully forgiven. As forgiven, the sinner is lifted up in Christ to a full relationship with God, whose grace leads the forgiven person to live in conformity to God's will.

For Luther this understanding was essential for living the Christian life. In his spiritual quest he discovered the saving love of Jesus Christ as a free gift to all who believe. He recognized that grace is not something to be earned, but instead something to be accepted in love. When we accept the grace of God and discover that God's justice is God's love, we recognize our own sinfulness and need for repentance.

In developing this insight, Luther disparaged the idea that practicing good works would help in any way a person's journey to salvation. A person was justified by faith alone, accepting the grace of Christ as a free gift. This grace covered the person in a cloak of Christ's grace that God alone would see.

Luther centered his teaching on the Scriptures as the source of God's revelation. Luther became extremely critical of the structures and teaching of the Church. He said that only in the Scriptures (*sola scriptura*) can a Christian find the teaching of what is needed for salvation. He rejected the teachings of the Church as authoritative, especially those of the popes and bishops in council. In order to get his message across, he wrote pamphlets, which were printed in the thousands, criticizing the Church.

Luther's teaching became popular through the development of his cate-chism, which was very effective in communicating the truths of the faith. Printed in 1539, Luther's catechism began with the commandments, fol-lowed by the Apostles' Creed, prayer, and the sacraments. Answers were worded as if instructing the father of a Christian family to teach his chil-dren the truths that were outlined. Luther's book was the first to be called a catechism—a more complex manual in the teacher's hands and a simpler version for the child. Luther's catechism also showed the way catechesis would be done in the world of print. He insisted on rote memorization of the text exactly as it appeared on the page so his teaching would remain intact. Memorization thus preceded analysis.

The Catholic Response to Luther

The official Catholic response to Luther's challenge was formulated at the Council of Trent (1545–1563). The Council of Trent taught that we are jus-tified by the redeeming grace won for us by the life, death, and resurrection of Jesus Christ. Christ's grace does not just cover us but renews us interi-orly so that we become new creations in Christ.

The council also taught that the Scriptures are the word of God, but are to be read in union with Catholic tradition. The magisterium of the Church was the authentic interpreter of Scripture and its meaning for Christian life.

At this council, the Church reaffirmed the basic teachings of the Church, taught that Scripture should be read in the context of Church life, and pro-duced a summary of the faith in the *Catechism of the Council of Trent*.

In order to disseminate Catholic teaching, the bishops called for the development of catechetical materials that would communicate it accurately. One of the main goals was to show how the Catholic understanding of the faith differed distinctly from that of Luther. Catholics countered Luther's catechism by producing texts with the same question-and-answer format.

Saint Peter Canisius, S.J. (1521–1597)

The most successful of the early Catholic catechisms were those written by Saint Peter Canisius. In 1555 he published a large catechism, the *Summary*

33

of Christian Doctrine. He followed this with a *Small Catechism* in 1556 that could be used by parish priests and students. It contained fifty-nine questions covering faith and the creed, hope and the Lord's Prayer, charity and the Ten Commandments, sacraments, and good works and the avoidance of sin. To the questions and answers, Peter added prayers for all occasions: morning and evening prayers, prayers for before and after meals, and a daily prayer for all needs. Peter's final catechism, *The Little Catechism for Catholics* (1558), written for young people, was his most popular—134 editions were published by 1597. Peter Canisius's catechisms would set the tone of catechesis in Germany for the next two hundred years.

CHAPTER 9

Catechesis in the United States, 1840–Present

The Reformation divided Christians into competing camps. The impact of the teachings of Martin Luther and later those of John Calvin (1509–1564) created divisions in European Christendom that led to decades of religious conflicts, ending with the Peace of Westphalia in 1648. These divisions are also reflected in the settlement of the eastern shore of the what was to become the United States. Protestant groups established early settlements such as Cape Cod in Massachusets.

If one were to draw a map of religion during the Colonial period and the early history of the United States, it would show a predominant influence of Protestant denominations. The principle English Catholic colony was established in Maryland, but it had to survive times of persecution and hostility from the predominant Protestant majority. After the American Revolution, active persecution ended, but the Catholic Church was a minority religion. Religious education was done primarily in the home. There was no system of Catholic education to support parents in handing on the faith.

The 1840s began a period of massive immigration from Europe to the United States. Millions of Catholics came from northern and later southern Europe seeking to gain the benefits promised in a land of opportunity. When they arrived, they discovered a different kind of religious landscape. Protestant agencies and school boards controlled the social system and the growing public school system. The school boards insisted on using the King James Bible in the schools, and when Catholics objected, they were ignored. The bishops of the United States decided to create the Catholic school system and other social structures that would support Catholic communities.

The bishops of the United States eventually hoped to create a unified English-speaking Church formed around a common catechism. This eventually led to the publication of the *Baltimore Catechism,* so named because it was approved at the Third Plenary Council in Baltimore in 1885. The *Baltimore Catechism* went through many revisions, the final major revision in 1941. The primary pedagogical method of the *Baltimore Catechism* was the memorization of questions and answers, and proficiency in religion was measured by the repetition of these answers in a classroom setting.

In a culture dominated by print media, learning was primarily an academic exercise. Academic values of precision, memorization of written formulas, and the ability to repeat what had been taught influenced the way religious education was carried out. And because the printed catechisms emerged in an atmosphere of argument between Catholics and Protestants, the tone of the early catechisms was apologetic—based on the notion that one must learn coherent arguments to defend the faith and to answer any objections that might come from other Christian groups and from the increasingly secularized world.

The strengths of printed catechisms were their ability to make accessible a great deal of information and the possibility to form a people around a single vocabulary of faith. Among the limitations was the temptation to see the educational task as ending with the memorization of written formulas and to ignore the need to internalize the knowledge in a way that touched the heart.

Catechesis was not limited to the classroom, however. While the formulas of the faith were learned in an abstract way in the classroom, active parishes offered a variety of ways for people to learn. Sermons at Sunday Mass, devotions such as the Rosary, and benedictions, novenas, missions by visiting priests, and processions of the whole parish on important feasts of the liturgical year rounded out Christian life. Social welfare was the concern of the Saint Vincent de Paul Society, and local credit unions provided ways for people to secure their resources and support one another.

While there may be some nostalgia for what was a viable culture of Catholicism, the times have changed. The parish is no longer the social center of life for Catholics in the United States. Devotions no longer bring out crowds in the evenings. The Church is competing with many religious traditions for the attention of the faithful. The situation of the Church today is in many ways similar to the church Ignatius of Loyola faced in the sixteenth century.

CHAPTER 10

Catechesis at the End of the Twentieth and the Beginning of the Twenty-first Centuries

As we view the social and religious situation at the beginning of the twenty-first century, we find many similarities with those the Church faced in the sixteenth century. In each case we see the breakdown of what people thought were steady, inviolable patterns of thought and social interaction. During the sixteenth century, the dislocations influenced all of society. Near the end of the twentieth and beginning of the twenty-first centuries, the dislocations reflected what was happening in society as well as the internal challenges within the Church.

The sixteenth century was an age of exploration and discovery that opened seemingly infinite horizons to the European imagination. Explorers and traders were discovering ancient civilizations that seemed more refined and wiser than those at home. Today a space station circles the globe, and unmanned missions are being sent to Mars. The Hubble telescope is sending pictures of galaxies colliding in distance space, and geneticists are exploring the interior universe of the human body. Every day, people see images of the religious plurality across the globe and, increasingly, in their neighborhoods and schools. All of this leads to questions about religious values and relationships to others.

The sixteenth century was also in the middle of a communications revolution. The invention of print made possible a new culture of learning and debate. Numerous editions of the Bible were being printed and circulated. Greek and Roman classical literature was being rediscovered as ancient manuscripts were brought out from the monasteries and printed for wide distribution. People reading the manuscripts were introduced to pagan ideas, and they became skeptical about the Christian worldview they had inherited. A growing literate population discovered that they were free to discover personally meaningful truths without being tied to the opinions of their elders.

Today the information revolution is even more staggering and intense. Through radio and television people witness world events. The growth of the Internet floods readers with a wealth of information almost impossible to digest. Structures of learning are increasingly horizontal; as young people are able to create new information networks, they are less dependent on schools and wisdom figures to guide their learning.

During the sixteenth century, people were concerned about personal salvation. The structures of Christendom that brought the Christian into the world in baptism and sent him or her on to God in the last rites were breaking down. Luther's challenge to Church authority led many people to question where they stood in relationship to God. As we will see in chapter 12, the "care of souls" was what Ignatius of Loyola thought to be his most important mission. He addressed the issues of religious identity and led people one-on-one to a close relationship with Jesus through the Spiritual Exercises.

Today the search for salvation, for personal meaning and fulfillment, is done in the context of a pluralistic society with many religious options. Many schools offer courses in comparative religion, and the tenets of Islam, Buddhism, Hinduism, and lesser-known religions are becoming more familiar to lay audiences. Teachings of many of these religious traditions are shuffled together in the eclectic collection of New Age beliefs. Of growing concern to Catholic bishops and educators is the indifference of many people toward religion of any kind.

Since the Second Vatican Council, the Church has begun to address the issue of how to catechize a world increasingly distracted by a vast hodgepodge of information. The first response has been a series of documents that have explored the Catholic tradition and re-visioned the catechetical agenda.

CHAPTER 11

Catechesis Since the Second Vatican Council

The Second Vatican Council met from 1962 to 1965. At the end of the council there was discussion about publishing a catechism similar to the *Catechism of the Council of Trent*. The bishops decided that publication of a complete catechism would be premature and that instead a catechetical directory would be published. This initiated a series of remarkable documents on the meaning and mission of catechesis that are shaping the way in which catechesis will be done in the twenty-first century.

Catechetical Documents

Following are brief summaries of eight of the most critical of these documents.

GENERAL CATECHETICAL DIRECTORY (1971)

The first of the catechetical documents published after the council was the "General Catechetical Directory" (GCD). The GCD shows the influence of the Second Vatican Council in two aspects: (1) its underlying principle is that of historical consciousness, and (2) it presents catechesis not in terms of carefully outlined truths to be memorized but as the product of historical development. The GCD helps locate catechesis as a ministry within the context of the ministry of the word. As the document states:

Revelation, therefore, consists of deed and words, the ones illuminating, and being illuminated by, the others. The ministry of the word should proclaim these deeds and words in such a way that the loftiest mysteries contained in them are further explained and communicated by it. In this way the ministry of the word not only recalls the revelation of God's wonders which was made in time and brought to perfection in Christ, but at the same time, and the light of this revelation, interprets human life in our age, the signs of the times, and the things of this world, for the plan of God works in these for the salvation of men.[7]

By situating catechesis within the ministry of the word, the GCD returned the understanding of the term *catechesis* to the ancient usage that broadens the catechetical dimension of nurturing the faith beyond the use of books to inform the mind The GCD calls for a return to the sources of Catholic tradition in Scripture and liturgy to help interpret human life in our age. It calls the catechist into dialogue with the world and to discover how God is working within the signs of the times for human salvation.

To Teach as Jesus Did (1972)

In 1972 the bishops of the United States, concerned with the direction of religious education, released the document "To Teach as Jesus Did" (TJD). TJD identifies the mission of catechesis as a lifelong process with the three dimensions of message, community, and service. The document also artic- ulates those areas in which the mission is to be carried out and sets an agenda for action.

The message unfolds the Revelation of God and his plan of salvation revealed in Jesus Christ. This is a living tradition handed on by the apostles under the direction of the Holy Spirit. The message calls Christians to faith.

Faith involves intellectual acceptance but also much more. Through faith men have a new vision of God, the world, and themselves. They must not only accept the Christian message but act on it, witnessing as individuals and as a community to all that Jesus said and did.[8]

Receiving the message calls us to live in community.

Community is the heart of Christian education not simply as a concept to be taught but as a reality to be lived. Through education, men must be moved to build community in all areas of life; they can do this best if they have learned the meaning of community by experiencing it. Formed by this experience, they are better able to build community in their families, their places of work, their neighborhoods, their nation, their world.[9]

Finally, all of this is done to prepare Christians to be of service to the Church and the world.

The experience of Christian community leads naturally to service. Christ gives His people different gifts not only for themselves but also for others. Each must serve the other for the good of all. The Church is a servant community in which those who hunger are to be filled; the ignorant are to be taught; the homeless to receive shelter; the sick cared for; the distressed consoled; the oppressed set free—all so that men may more fully realize their human potential and more readily enjoy life with God now and eternally.[10]

TJD emphasizes first the importance of teaching adults. "Consequently the continuing education of adults is situated not at the periphery of the Church's educational mission but at its center."[11]

BASIC TEACHINGS FOR CATHOLIC EDUCATION (1973)

The bishops of the United States published "Basic Teachings for Catholic Religious Education" (BT) in 1973. This document was published to balance the focus on experiential process of faith formation with a concern that Catholic doctrine not be ignored. While systematically listing the teachings of the Catholic faith, the bishops emphasized the importance of prayer.

The People of God have always been a praying people. Religious educators, who are mature in the faith and faithful to this tradition, will teach prayer. This teaching will take place through experiences of prayer, through the example of prayer, and through the learning of common prayers. Religious education, at home or in the classroom, given by a teacher who values prayer, will provide both the instruction and the experience.[12]

"Basic Teachings" also emphasizes the centrality of the liturgy for growth in the Christian life. "Liturgy itself educates. It teaches, it forms community, it forms the individual. It makes possible worship of God and a social apostolate to men."[13]

In its third theme, BT emphasizes the importance of familiarity with the Bible.

> Religious education should encourage love and respect for the Scriptures. This will happen as one is gradually introduced to the Scriptures and given a background knowledge which will prepare him for reading and understanding them. At an appropriate level, each one should have his own copy of the Bible.[14]

The BT also stresses that catechesis is about initiating people into a faith community and strengthening the bonds of community. The meaning of the *Basic Teachings* is lived out in service to God and others.

ON EVANGELIZATION IN THE MODERN WORLD (1975)

In 1974, Pope Paul VI convoked a synod of bishops to discuss the issue of evangelization. Pope Paul VI was concerned that the Church's message of God's love for the world was not being adequately shared both within and beyond the Church. The bishops encouraged the pope to summarize their discussions and to give pastoral guidance and direction for the Church. This the pope did in 1975 with the release of the encyclical "On Evangelization in the Modern World" (EN). In it, he stressed the centrality of evangelization in the life of the Church.

> Evangelizing is in fact the grace and vocation proper to the Church, her deepest identity. She exists in order to evangelize, that is to say in order to preach and to teach, to be the channel of the life of grace, to reconcile sinners to God, and to perpetuate Christ's sacrifice at the Mass, which is the memorial of his death and glorious Resurrection.[15]

Evangelization demands that the Church be faithful to the message being proclaimed and to the people who are to receive it. People need to hear that God loves them through the life and ministry of Jesus Christ. This must be heard as a liberating message not only in individual life but in social life as well. Evangelization is possible only when the Church is aware of the need for renewal and reform both within the Church and in society at large.

Sharing the Light of Faith (1978)

In 1978, the bishops of the United States responded to the "General Catechetical Directory" with the National Catechetical Directory (NCD) entitled "Sharing the Light of Faith," a pastoral and practical document on the norms and guidelines for teaching religion in the context of the United States. "Sharing the Light of Faith" continues in the direction of stressing how important catechesis is as a lifelong process.

> While aiming to enrich the faith life of individuals in their particular stages of development, every form of catechesis is oriented in some way to the catechesis of adults, who are capable of a full response to God's word. Catechesis is a lifelong process for the individual and a constant and concerted pastoral activity of the Christian community.[16]

The NCD covers the four main components of catechesis: message, community, worship, and service. It provides an overview of Catholic teaching with clear directions for catechetical practice. Sensitive to the issues of human development, the NCD stresses the need to adapt to the specific ages, experiences, cultures, and circumstances of individuals and communities. It especially stresses the need of catechesis to address concerns in Catholic social teaching.

> Catechesis for justice, mercy, and peace is a continuing process which concerns every person and every age. It first occurs in the family by word and by example. It is continued in a systematic way by Church institutions, parishes, schools, trade unions, political parties, and the like. This catechesis is an integral part of parish catechetical programs. It should also be an integral part of the curriculum and environment of Catholic schools. It is desirable that courses for children and youth be complemented by programs for parents.[17]

On Catechesis in Our Time (1979)

In 1977, the International Synod of Bishops met in Rome to study catechesis of children and youth. Pope John Paul II summarized the findings of their meeting in 1999 in the apostolic exhortation "On Catechesis in Our Time" (CT). Through this exhortation John Paul II presents a vision of catechesis for the universal church.

CT describes catechesis as a moment in evangelization.

The one message—the Good News of salvation—that has been heard once or hundreds of times and has been accepted with the heart, is in catechesis probed unceasingly by reflection and systematic study, by awareness of its repercussions on one's personal life—an awareness for even greater commitment—and by inserting it into an organic and harmonious whole, namely Christian living in society and the world.[18]

"On Catechesis in Our Time" also emphasizes the ecclesial dimension of catechesis.

Catechesis is intimately bound up with the whole of the Church's life. Not only her geographical extension and numerical increase but also even more her inner growth and correspondence with God's plan depend essentially on catechesis.[19]

The more the Church, whether on the local or the universal level, gives catechesis priority over other works and undertakings the results of which would be more spectacular, the more she finds in catechesis a strengthening of her internal life as a community of believers and of her external activity as a missionary church. As the twentieth century draws to a close, the Church is bidden by God and by events—each of them a call from him—to renew her trust in catechetical activity as a prime aspect of her mission. She is bidden to offer catechesis her best resources in people and energy, without sparing effort, toil or material means, in order to organize it better and to train qualified personnel. This is not mere human calculation; it is an attitude of faith. And an attitude of faith always has reference to the faithfulness of God, who never fails to respond.[20]

THE CATECHISM OF THE CATHOLIC CHURCH

At the Extraordinary Synod of Bishops gathered to celebrate the twentieth anniversary of the Second Vatican Council in 1985, the bishops made a formal proposal that a new catechism be written that would support the work of catechesis throughout the world. Pope John Paul II appointed a commission of twelve cardinals to supervise the writing of the catechism. Drafts of the proposed catechism were sent to Catholic bishops worldwide. They responded with 24,000 suggested amendments that were taken under consideration by the commission.

In the apostolic constitution *Fidei depositum* issued in 1992, Pope John Paul II introduced the *Catechism of the Catholic Church* written to serve as a norm for teaching the faith. The *Catechism* is designed to provide writers of local catechisms a "sure and authentic reference text for teaching Catholic doctrine." With the aid of such a reference the faithful could deepen their knowledge of "the unfathomable riches of salvation. Ecumenical initiatives would be strengthened as the faithful were supported in the knowledge of what the Church teaches. The *Catechism* presents "the content and wondrous harmony of the Catholic faith."

The *Catechism of the Catholic Church* is an essential summary of Catholic teaching on faith and morals. It is to be a point of reference for national and diocesan catechisms. Its presentation of the faith is declarative, meant to be a positive and objective presentation of Catholic teaching.

In order to carry out their duty as teachers of the faith, the bishops of the United States established the Office of the Catechism and set up a voluntary review process of all catechetical materials to assess whether they are written in conformity with the *Catechism*.

General Directory for Catechesis (1997)

In 1997 the Congregation of the Clergy published the *General Directory for Catechesis (GDC)*. The *GDC* is addressed principally to the Catholic bishops, episcopal conferences, and, in a general way, to those who are responsible for catechetical ministry on the local level. With the publication of the *Catechism of the Catholic Church* and other catechetical documents, such as those reviewed here, a revision of *General Catechetical Directory* was needed. In the revision, two principal requirements were kept in mind: (1) catechesis must be seen within the context of evangelization, and (2) the revised document must use content of the faith as summarized in the *Catechism of the Catholic Church*.

The *GDC* discusses catechesis in the context of evangelization. It lays out the norms and criteria for presenting the gospel message. And it presents the *Catechism of the Catholic Church* as the reference point for transmitting the faith and for preparing catechists at the local level.

The *GDC* also discusses the pedagogy of the faith in light of God's gradual revelation of himself over time, also taking into account what human sciences have taught us about the learning process. The *GDC* covers the diverse situations and contexts in which catechesis is done and the necessity that all catechesis be conducted in a way that respects the need for inculturation. The *GDC* calls attention to the necessity of the local church to promote, organize, and oversee catechetical activities at the local level.

GDC on the Source of Catechesis

Catechesis finds its source in the word of God as expressed in Scripture and Tradition. The Church carries the responsibility to transmit this sacred "deposit of faith" from generation to generation. Just as the Son of God "… emptied himself, taking the form of a slave, coming in human likeness," (Philippians 4:7) God's Word is shared with the world in human words and actions. Words are not static but dynamic; their meanings shift and they need to be interpreted continually. Guided by the Holy Spirit, the Church contemplates the word she has received, guards its true meaning, and faithfully proclaims it for a new generation.

GDC on Criteria for Effective Catechesis

The *GDC* describes a number of criteria for effective catechesis. An authentic catechesis is centered on the person of Jesus Christ, especially attending to the Trinitarian dimension of the relationship of Jesus the Son of God sent by his Father for our salvation in the Holy Spirit. Jesus came to proclaim the Kingdom of God, God's offer of salvation to all, which leads to human liberation. The Church is the context in which catechesis takes place; it is the Church's mission to proclaim the meaning of Jesus and the Kingdom of God in time. If the message of the Gospel is to be transmitted with clarity and integrity, the catechist takes into consideration the cultural context in which it is being proclaimed. Finally, the message must be proclaimed in a comprehensive way so that the whole of the Gospel in all if its implications can shape human life.

GDC on the Fundamental Tasks of Catechesis

Catechesis has four fundamental tasks.

The first is promotion of knowledge that leads to Christian faith. This is not simply factual knowledge about the faith, but a sharing of faith in such a way that there is coherence between the information and the transformation of the believer in Christ. Catechesis does this by nourishing the life of faith in the believer and preparing the believer to become a witness to Christ in the world.

The second fundamental task is liturgical education. The purpose of catechesis is to help believers become full, active, and conscious participants in the liturgy. This is done by educating the believer "for prayer, for thanksgiving, for repentance, for praying with confidence, for community spirit, for understanding correctly the meaning of the creeds."

The third fundamental task of catechesis is support of the process by which people learn and celebrate the faith. Catechesis helps create disciples who are ready to make decisions in the light of a growing personal relationship with Jesus Christ. Guided by the Ten Commandments and Jesus' teaching in the Beatitudes, the disciple learns to make choices to care for self, others, and the needs of the world. Catechesis prepares the disciple for evangelization, as true evangelization involves showing the world through actions what it means to live out the implications of Christian social teaching.

Finally, the process of catechesis culminates in the life of prayer. The disciple learns to pray as Jesus did, praying the Lord's Prayer, the prayer that Jesus taught us. The disciple learns to pray prayers of adoration, praise, thanksgiving, friendly confidence, supplication, and awe for God's glory.

When catechesis is permeated by a climate of prayer, the assimilation of the entire Christian life reaches its summit. This climate is especially necessary when the catechumen and those to be catechized are confronted with the more demanding aspects of the Gospel and when they feel weak or when they discover the mysterious action of God in their lives.

Summary

The catechetical documents help to establish the parameters for catechesis in the twenty-first century. They emphasize that catechesis is meant to help the disciple become more closely related to Jesus Christ, fed by the sources of Scripture and Tradition, which helps the believer serve the Kingdom of God and be a sign of the grace of God in the world. This is what Ignatius of Loyola taught in his day. We will now look at Ignatius's contribution and the way in which Ignatian spirituality can be a source of enlightenment and discipline for catechesis today.

CHAPTER 12

Ignatius of Loyola and Catechesis

Ignatius was the youngest of thirteen children born to a noble family in the Basque country in Spain. His family had many connections with the political and social elite, and they sent him to be trained as a courtier in the household of a duke. Ignatius learned that he was expected to serve society, to face danger courageously, and to endure hardship. He learned how to be courteous, to control his emotions, and to practice the traditional piety of Christian Spain.

In his autobiography, Ignatius admits that he also learned the negative side of the courtier's life. He was touchy about anything that might challenge his personal honor. He was proud of his long blond hair and always dressed in the latest fashion. Extramarital affairs were an accepted part of life. While practicing the traditional piety of Spain, he did not connect his spiritual practices with his moral choices or lifestyle.

Ignatius was well trained and ambitious. He had some success as a diplomat and was conscientious in carrying out his military duties. When the French attacked the castle he was assigned to in Pamplona, Spain, Ignatius persuaded the badly outnumbered garrison to preserve their honor and continue to fight. The garrison followed his lead until a cannonball shattered both of his legs. With Ignatius severely wounded and out of command, the garrison promptly surrendered. The French treated Ignatius with respect, returning him to his home in Loyola.

Recovery and Transformation

Ignatius spent months in recovery, undergoing a painful operation to break his legs and reset them. As the bones healed, Ignatius still had a limp, so to fix the twist in the bones of one leg, they were once again broken and reset. During this long and trying period, it's not surprising that Ignatius became bored. He asked for something to read, hoping to lose himself in stories of great quests and fervent romance. The only books available, however, were a book about the lives of the saints and a four-volume set on the life of Jesus.

As he read those books, Ignatius's perception of the "heroic life" changed drastically. He resonated especially with the stories of Saint Francis of Assisi and Saint Dominic. He found that his daydreams about romance left him hollow, while daydreams about serving God brought great joy, peace, and hope. Thus he began to discern what hopes and dreams came from God and were worthy of following, and what hopes would lead to illusion and dissatisfaction.

By the time he had recovered from his wounds, Ignatius decided that he, too, could lead a heroic life of service to God, as had his heroes Saint Francis and Saint Dominic. He resumed his life with the same ambitious drive as before, only now it was redirected toward the benefit of God's kingdom.

Making a Decision for God

Once Ignatius decided to give himself to God's service, he became determined to do penance for his sinful life. He traveled to the Benedictine monastery of Montserrat, Spain, as the first stage of a pilgrimage that he hoped would eventually take him to Jerusalem. At Montserrat he made a general confession of his sins and dedicated his life to Mary, the mother of God. Ignatius then spent a number of months in the town of Manresa. He went through periods of haunting scruples and near despair over his memory of past sins. He also had a deep experience of God's presence and realized that this presence permeated all of life and creation. He painstakingly recorded his spiritual journey; these written thoughts eventually became the first draft of the *Spiritual Exercises,* which would become a classic text on spiritual direction.

At Manresa Ignatius had a deep experience of God's loving presence in the world, fulfilling and upholding him. The memory of this positive experience stayed with him the rest of his life and profoundly influenced his vision of the world.

> The Ignatian vision of the world . . . flows from his becoming aware that the whole universe is in movement toward God. Without knowing it, the world proclaims its Lord and evolves toward a fuller participation in the divine glory. Thus it is a mirror revealing God's power and splendor to us, who by means of it can come to know God better, and praise and love him better, and be self-fulfilled or happy doing this. This outlook on the world touches also the personal life of Ignatius and places it within this universal movement. The substantial changes which his experience of the mystery of God introduces into his life amply testify to this. The human creature, a conscious and free creature, ought to assume the responsibility for this return of the world to the Father.[21]

Ignatius then made a pilgrimage to Jerusalem, where he hoped to spend the rest of his life. Jerusalem was then under Muslim rule, and Catholics were allowed only a limited mission. Ignatius's enthusiastic piety made the priest in charge of the Jerusalem Church quite nervous, and the priest sent Ignatius home.

Back in Spain, Ignatius returned to school to learn Latin, a language he needed to continue studies at the university level. He shared the process of the Spiritual Exercises with others, which brought him the attention of the Spanish Inquisition. Finally, the authorities told him that he must be ordained in order to continue to practice spiritual direction. So Ignatius went to Paris to study for ordination. In Paris, he met and inspired the seven men who would join him to form the Company of Jesus, the Jesuits. The small community of men at first hoped to go to Jerusalem, but the political situation made it impossible. They then decided to go to Rome and offer their services to the pope. In 1546, the Jesuits were given approval by Rome to form a new religious order, the Company of Jesus. Ignatius was elected their first superior.

Influence of the Exercises

Ignatius continued to practice and conduct the Spiritual Exercises. The exercises guide the exercitant on a silent retreat of about thirty days, during which, for four or more hours each day, he follows a series of set meditations. The retreat master is the guide; the director of the retreat is God.

The content of the Exercises follows the basic structure of Christian belief as found in the Bible. The stories in the Gospels are emphasized, and the material is divided into four "weeks." The first week focuses on the theme of creation. The exercitant meditates on the beauty of creation and the reason our view of creation is disoriented and can lead us away from God. The exercitant meditates especially on the enormity of human sin. During the second week, the exercitant meditates on the hidden life and public ministry of Jesus. These meditations give the exercitant opportunity to reflect on his own life of discipleship. During the third week, the passion and death of Jesus are the subjects of meditation. The meditation for the fourth week centers upon the story of Jesus' Resurrection.

Throughout the four weeks, exercitants are learning to discern God's will for their lives. They practice the process that Ignatius discovered as he reflected on the life of Christ and the lives of the saints. The exercitants are to be especially attentive to their own inclinations and motivations. These are keys to discerning who God is calling them to be. They also become more aware of how spirits of destruction and disorientation are working in their lives.

Practicing the Spiritual Exercises helps exercitants develop a positive appreciation of God's presence in creation. The Exercises cultivate the visual and other sensory imagination in prayer. As participants reflect upon scenes from the gospels, using imagination to enter the stories as characters, they learn to grow in an affective relationship with Jesus, his family, friends, and followers.

The Exercises were Ignatius's response to the cultural dislocation taking place in Europe during the sixteenth century. He responded by helping people grow in a more intimate relationship with Jesus Christ and discern ways in which they could be of greater service to God and the Church.

For Ignatius, the sign that someone was ready to be transformed by Christ was that person's recognition that serving God meant serving God's creation. Ignatius asked that person to respond to three questions: What have I done for Christ? What am I now doing for Christ? What ought I do for Christ?

Ignatius was convinced that we experience the presence of God in the midst of the world. He urged everyone to pray for the grace to reflect deeply on one's life and for the gratitude to be thankful for these blessings.

Because it is based in the Spiritual Exercises, Ignatian spirituality is grounded in intense gratitude and reverence. It begins with and continually reverts to the awareness of the presence and power and care of God everywhere, for everyone, and at all times.[22]

A Spirituality of Service

Ignatian spirituality leads participants to serve the Kingdom of God. Christians are called to surrender their wills and faculties to God in the sense of dedicating their freedom, strength, and skills to the service of God. The grace that we receive from God empowers us to serve in ways God wants us to serve.

> Ignatian spirituality is at the service of the gospel and the reign of God; it is a means by which the word of God may come alive and be made flesh. Further interpretation and exploration from different points of view, therefore, serves to illustrate once again the wealth of the gospel and its continuing power to enrich and transform lives across a wide spectrum of people and of diverse spiritual traditions in very different circumstances of time and place.[23]

Ignatius's vision for his new community was that it should find God in the midst of the world. In his time, religious communities spent long hours every day in prayer. He was concerned that spending too much time at prayer interfered with their mission to find God in everyday life.

> [Ignatius's] travels, especially when unaccompanied, catered for his contemplative longings. Drawing on his own experience during his years of study, he once advised the Jesuit students in Portugal, who were inordinately attached to long hours of prayer that interfered with their studies, to find God everywhere and in everything:

in their conversation, their walks, all that they see, taste and hear, in their actions, since His Divine Majesty is truly in all things by his presence, power and essence. . . . This is an excellent practice to prepare us for the great visitations of our Lord even when our prayers are rather short.[24]

Ignatius of Loyola's vision for helping people in confusing times was to give them the method they needed to form an intimate relationship with Jesus Christ and one another. He emphasized the beauty of creation as God's gift to us. He taught people to use their imaginations in contemplation and prayer. He was adamant in teaching that service to God is expressed in service to others. These are values that are developed in *Finding God: Our Response to God's Gifts.*

CHAPTER 13

Finding God: Our Response to God's Gifts

The desire for God is written in the human heart.

Catechism of the Catholic Church, 27

As in the time of Ignatius of Loyola, people today are living in a confusion of rapid communication and cultural diversity. In the catechetical documents issued since the Second Vatican Council, the Church has emphasized the dynamic nature of catechesis to help disciples form a close relationship with Jesus. The Church teaches that the aim of catechesis is "to put people, not only in touch, but also in communion and intimacy with Jesus Christ" (GDC 80). *Finding God: Our Response to God's Gifts* has been created to help fulfill this aim.

Finding God: Our Response to God's Gifts was born out of the decision of Loyola Press to create a catechetical program reflecting the contribution that Ignatian spirituality could make to helping people grow in Christian life. The religious education of youth was a great concern for Ignatius. In his autobiography he described how, soon after his studies in Paris and his return to Loyola, Spain, he taught children about Jesus.

> As soon as [Ignatius] arrived, he made up his mind to teach the catechism daily to children. But his brother made strenuous objection to this, declaring that nobody would come. The pilgrim answered that one would be

57

enough. But after he began, many came faithfully to hear him, even his brother.[25]

In the *Constitutions of the Society of Jesus,* Ignatius describes the mission of the society as one

> founded chiefly for this purpose: to strive especially for the defense and propagation of the faith and for the progress of souls in Christian life and doctrine, by means of public preaching, lectures and any other ministration of the world of God, and further by means of the Spiritual Exercises, the education of children and uneducated persons in Christianity, and the spiritual consolation of Christ's faithful through hearing confessions and administering the other sacraments.[26]

When a number of Jesuits were called to the Council of Trent (1543–1565) to take part in the proceedings as theological advisors to the bishops in council, Ignatius instructed them to take time each day to teach children.

To the Fathers at the Council of Trent

> While in Trent, ours should try to remain together in some reputable district. And what they should especially seek to accomplish for God's greater glory is to preach, hear confessions, lecture, instruct children, give good example, visit the poor in the hospitals, exhort the neighborhood according to the amount of talent which each is conscious of possessing, so as to move as many as possible to prayer and devotion.[27]

> You should teach [children] for some suitable time according to convenient arrangements, which will vary in different places. Begin with the first rudiments, and explain them in keeping with the needs of your hearers. When you finish with such instruction recite some prayers for the council. [28]

Like Saint Peter Canisius, many early Jesuits were quite active in religious education, taking advantage of all the media available to proclaim God's word.

One of the ways, though, in which the new orders of the sixteenth century might be seen as innovative is in their use of mass media and techniques of salesmanship and publicity which we associate with modernity, the media and mass culture. For example, Jesuits in Germany, led by Peter Canisius (1521–1597), were phenomenally successful in promoting their message and in winning over opinion in large tracts of the German lands: they composed catechisms for the use of schoolmasters, published plays, poems and hymns, tracts and brochures conveying the themes they wanted to put across, set up and directed sodalities, organized pilgrimages, and carried out missions deep in Protestant territory.[29]

The early Jesuits also used music to catechize the people.

It was with the help of tunes that children came into their own. Polanco reported with happened in Gandia in 1554. One of the Jesuit scholastics, accompanied by two boys, walked through the streets ringing a little bell. The boys meanwhile sang parts of the catechism "in a sweet melody." As the children gathered behind their three leaders, they were led to a church, where classes were taught and the tunes learned. The tunes and lyrics became so popular that "day and night in the whole town nothing was sung by both adults and children but 'Christian Doctrine'"—by craftsmen and day laborers in the town, by farmers in their fields, by mothers, who had learned it from their children, in the homes. The lessons were taught in the church daily in the winter and once a week in the summer, sometimes to as many as four hundred children. Those who did particularly well received prizes, but the enthusiasm was so great that often seventy or eighty prizes had to be awarded.[30]

In the spirit of Ignatius and the early Jesuits, Loyola Press has developed *Finding God: Our Response to God's Gifts* as a catechetical series to serve as the foundation for total parish catechesis.

.

CHAPTER 14

Developing
Finding God:
Our Response
to God's Gifts

In developing *Finding God: Our Response to God's Gifts* Loyola Press listened to catechetical leaders from all over the country who expressed a desire for materials that would enable catechists to bring the Catholic faith alive for those they teach. *Finding God: Our Response to God's Gifts* reflects a vision for catechesis that contains elements of the Ignatian approach and is grounded in the *General Directory for Catechesis* and the *Catechism of the Catholic Church.*

Finding God: Our Response to God's Gifts is based on authentic faith formation and the belief that effective catechesis:

~ reflects the love of the Father, Son, and Holy Spirit

~ is centered on the person of Jesus Christ and his proclamation of the Kingdom of God

~ proclaims the liberating good news of salvation through Jesus Christ

~ leads the Christian into the world in mission and action, in service to the kingdom

~ addresses the needs of the culture in which it is presented

~ invites individuals to reflect on personal experience in light of growing in relationship with God

~ leads to full, conscious, and active participation in the liturgical life of the Church

~ is permeated by a climate of prayer and nurtures a faith that is translated into prayer

Finding God: Our Response to God's Gifts is an authentic expression of the Catholic faith, found to be in conformity with the *Catechism of the Catholic Church* by the Ad Hoc Committee to Oversee the Use of the *Catechism of the Catholic Church*. It has an Imprimatur from the Archdiocese of Chicago. The program was written in harmony with the Church's doctrine and traditions "which are safeguarded by the bishops who teach with a unique authority."[31]

CHAPTER 15

Distinguishing Features of *Finding God:* *Our Response to God's Gifts*

Finding God: Our Response to God's Gifts reflects the goals of catechesis as outlined in the catechetical documents published since the Second Vatican Council. It integrates Scripture and Tradition in every session, reflects the value of Catholic social teaching, and shows the links between catechesis and liturgy. *Finding God: Our Response to God's Gifts* also clearly presents Catholic moral teaching and helps the participants to pray from within the truths they are learning.

Scripture and Tradition

In his apostolic exhortation "On Catechesis in Our Time," John Paul II emphasized the importance of catechesis drawing its content from Scripture and Tradition.

> Catechesis will always draw its content from the living source of the word of God transmitted in Tradition and the Scriptures, for sacred Tradition and

sacred Scripture make up a single sacred deposit of the word of God, which is entrusted to the Church.[32]

While applauding the increased reading of Scripture as a positive development in religious education, the GDC also cautions that Scripture is too often being taught without reference to Tradition.

[I]n much catechesis, indeed, reference to Sacred Scripture is virtually exclusive and unaccompanied by sufficient reference to the Church's long experience and reflection,(Cf. CT 27b), acquired in the course of her two-thousand-year history. (*GDC* 30)

Scripture is the foundation for understanding the doctrine that is taught in each session of *Finding God: Our Response to God's Gifts.* The main Scripture reference uses a story or other passage from the Old Testament or New Testament to introduce the theme of the session. A second, shorter passage, "Reading God's Word," supports the main theme and gives an accessible Scripture quote that can be memorized. The "inter-relation of Sacred Scripture, Tradition and the Magisterium, each according to 'its proper mode'" are presented in a harmonious way that enriches the catechetical transmission of the faith (*GDC* 30).

Catholic Social Teaching

In 1998, the United States bishops released the document *Sharing Catholic Social Teaching: Challenges and Directions,* which outlined seven areas of Catholic social teaching to be addressed in religious education programs. *Finding God: Our Response to God's Gifts* supports and promotes these seven principles of Catholic social teaching.

1. LIFE AND DIGNITY OF THE HUMAN PERSON
The Catholic Church teaches us that all human life is sacred and that all people must be treated with dignity. As Catholics, we strive to respect and value people over material goods. We are called to ask whether our actions as a society respect or threaten the life and dignity of the human person. Our belief in the life and dignity of the human person is the foundation of our moral vision.

2. **CALL TO FAMILY, COMMUNITY, AND PARTICIPATION**
   Participation in family and community is central to our faith and to a healthy society. As the central social institution of our society, the family must be supported and strengthened. From this foundation people participate in society, fostering a community spirit and promoting the well-being of all, especially the poor and vulnerable.

3. **RIGHTS AND RESPONSIBILITIES**
   The Catholic Church teaches that every person has a right to life as well as a right to those things required for human decency. As Catholics, it is our responsibility to protect these fundamental human rights in order to achieve a healthy society. The only way to protect human dignity and to live in a healthy community is for each of us to accept our responsibility to protect those rights in our own interactions.

4. **OPTION FOR THE POOR AND VULNERABLE**
   In our world, many people are very rich, while at the same time, many are extremely poor. As Catholics, we are called to pay special attention to the needs of the poor. We can follow Jesus' example by making a specific effort to defend and promote the dignity of the poor and vulnerable and meet their immediate material needs.

5. **THE DIGNITY OF WORK AND THE RIGHTS OF WORKERS**
   The Catholic Church teaches that the basic rights of workers must be respected: the right to productive work, to fair wages, to private property, to organize and join unions, and to pursue economic opportunity. Moreover, Catholics believe that the economy is meant to serve people, not the other way around. More than being just a way to make a living, work is an important way in which we participate in God's creation.

6. **SOLIDARITY**
   Because God is our Father, we are all brothers and sisters with the responsibility to care for one another. Solidarity is the attitude that leads Christians to share spiritual and material goods. Solidarity unites rich and poor, weak and strong, and helps to create a society that recognizes that we all live in an interdependent world.

7. CARE FOR GOD'S CREATION

God is the creator of all people and all things, and he wants us to enjoy his creation. The responsibility to care for all that God has made is a requirement of our faith. We are called to make the moral and ethical choices that protect the ecological balance of creation, both locally and worldwide.

In *Finding God: Our Response to God's Gifts* these concepts of Catholic social teaching are integrated into each session. Each session plan tells the catechist which of these principles will be addressed in that session. The participants discover how what they have learned about God's love for them is expressed in acting in a socially responsible way toward others.

Liturgy in *Finding God: Our Response to God's Gifts*

The *General Directory for Catechesis* addresses concerns about the lack of integration between catechesis and liturgy. Among these concerns are: a lack of attention to liturgical symbols and rites, catechetical courses with little or no connection with the liturgical year, and the deemphasis of liturgical celebrations in catechetical programs. (GDC 30)

Catechesis helps disciples prepare for the sacraments by promoting a deeper understanding and experience of the liturgy. It helps to explain the context of the prayers, the meaning of signs and gestures. It helps the disciple learn to participate actively in the liturgy and to acquire the skills of contemplation and silence. (GDC 71)

In *Finding God: Our Response to God's Gifts* the sacraments of initiation are a central focus throughout the program. Further attention is given to the Sacraments of Penance and the Eucharist, especially in grades two and five. In the course of the program, all the sacraments are treated at ever-deepening levels to help the participants understand their importance and to prepare them for deeper participation.

Throughout the program, "Links to Liturgy" show the relation of doctrine to liturgical action. Seasonal sessions guide the catechist through the major seasons of the liturgical year: Advent, Christmas, Lent, Easter, and Pentecost and the Feast of All Saints.

All members of the parish are given opportunities for meditation and contemplative prayer throughout the program. As their personal prayer life deepens and their relationship with Jesus is nurtured, children have the opportunity to bring skills of contemplation and silence to their participation in the liturgy.

Morality

The person who follows Jesus must in turn imitate the life of Jesus. In *Finding God: Our Response to God's Gifts* participants are led to cooperate with God in a life of inner transformation, learning to make concrete decisions based on the Sermon on the Mount and the Ten Commandments. (In the Sermon on the Mount, Jesus shares the fundamental teachings for all who are called to serve the Kingdom of God. The Ten Commandments are foundational principles by which we live for God and others. *GDC 85*)

The principles for making moral decisions are presented throughout *Finding God: Our Response to God's Gifts* The Ten Commandments and the Beatitudes are explored especially in grade 4. The steps for making moral decisions, the sinful consequences of disobeying God's commandments, and the steps in reconciliation with God and others in the Sacrament of Penance are shared in ways that are relevant and meaningful.

Prayer in *Finding God: Our Response to God's Gifts*

Prayer is the culmination and fruit of all study. Christian prayer gives to the Father adoration, praise, and thanksgiving; expresses confidence in his love for us; voices supplication; and offers awe for his glory.

Jesus gave us the model of Christian prayer in the Lord's Prayer. Each time we pray the Lord's Prayer we summarize the entire Gospel.

The *General Directory for Catechesis* notes

> When catechesis is permeated by a climate of prayer, the assimilation of the entire Christian life reaches its summit. This climate is especially necessary when the catechumen and those to be catechized are confronted with the more demanding aspects of the Gospel and when they feel weak or when they discover the mysterious action of God in their lives. (*GDC 85*)

Finding God: Our Response to God's Gifts invites the catechist to create a climate of prayer for every session. Throughout the program, the catechist's presentation of the truths of the Catholic faith will take place within the context of a prayerful relationship with God. This reflects the Catholic understanding that faith formation "includes more than instruction: it is an apprenticeship" (GDC 67). In this apprenticeship, the catechist is called to mentor children into the Catholic way of life, including the practice of prayer. Since we mentor by doing, catechists will have a natural opportunity to pray with the children at specific moments in every session.

The first opportunity, near the beginning of the session, invites children to become aware of God's presence. This prayer of petition invites them to ask for God's help on their faith journey.

After the children have explored Scripture and Tradition, the catechist prays with the participants, using a guided reflection that flows from the focus of the session. Through these reflective prayer experiences, the catechist invites the children to enter into sacred time and space, engage in conversation with the Lord, and recognize his presence in their daily lives. Reflective prayer uses thought, imagination, emotion, and desire to deepen the participants' faith, foster a conversion of heart, and strengthen their will to follow Jesus (cf. CCC 2708). Experiences of reflective prayer also give the participants opportunities to take to heart the basic prayers of the Catholic Church.

Finally, when they are about to be sent forth to act on what they have learned, the children are given an opportunity to offer a prayer of gratitude that is related to what they have just learned about their faith.

St. Paul considered prayer to be of such importance that he instructed the Church to "pray without ceasing" (1 Thessalonians 5:17). You can help participants to "pray without ceasing" by helping them understand that prayer is "a vital and personal relationship with the living and true God" (CCC 2558) and that God invites them to live every moment of every day with an awareness of this relationship.

Conclusion

Finding God: Our Response to God's Gifts is carefully crafted to introduce the participants to the Christian way of life. It is designed to help people grow in a close relationship with Jesus Christ as he leads us to the Father. Christians are called to participate with the Church in service to the Kingdom of God, service that is expressed in caring for the world.

Christians of every generation have responded in ever-deepening ways to sharing the Good News of salvation in Jesus Christ. *Finding God: Our Response to God's Gifts* distills much of this wisdom through the lens of Ignatian spirituality. The ultimate goal of this program is to help people grow in relationship with God and one another.

Overview of Themes Central to Ignatian Spirituality and to the *General Directory for Catechesis*

Richard J. Hauser, S.J.
Creighton University

Listed below are seven major themes of Ignatian spirituality (IS) drawn primarily from Ignatius's booklet the *Spiritual Exercises*. The theme is presented and then related to a similar theme in the *General Directory for Catechesis* (GDC). There is great compatibility between the two approaches to spirituality.

Christ-Centered and Trinitarian: *Ad Majorem Dei Gloriam*

IS: The touchstone of Ignatian spirituality is the *Spiritual Exercises*. The grace sought in most meditations of the Exercises is "greater interior knowledge of Christ in order to love him more intensely and follow him more closely." Meditations center upon the kingdom of Christ, with Christ serving the kingdom of the Father.

GDC: Goal of catechesis presented throughout is communion with Jesus Christ: "The definitive aim of catechesis is to put people not only in touch with but also in communion and intimacy with Jesus Christ" (80). Trinitarian Christocentricity is called for throughout the document: "every mode of presentation must always be christo-trinitarian: Through Christ to the Father in the Holy Spirit." (100)

Experience-Centered: Finding God in All Things

IS: The goal of Ignatian spirituality is always a personal experience of the love of Christ. Ignatius assumes that the experience of spiritual consolation will accompany a faithful making of the thirty-day retreat. Outside the retreat Ignatius looks for a consciousness of the Spirit's presence as a sign of living in God in daily life. Daily exercises of examining conscience are encouraged to examine whether actions are rooted in Christ. Growing in a personal relationship with Christ practitioners of Ignatian spirituality attempt to become "contemplatives in action" by being rooted in God in every activity.

GDC: Human experience is the starting point for all catechetics: "Interpreting and illuminating experience with the data of faith is a constant task of catechetical pedagogy" (153). The GDC is concerned with learning the content of faith, the deposit of faith, but the final goal is never memorization but always conversion and communion with Jesus.

Person-Centered

IS: Ignatian spirituality is always adapted to the spiritual state of the individual making the retreat or being guided through spiritual direction. The assumption is that God is working within the individual, hence the goal is recognizing this work. Ignatian spirituality is never a superimposed construct of spiritual ideals forced on the individual. Ignatius assumes that the Spiritual Exercises will always be given one-on-one. The individually directed retreat movement respects this dynamic.

GDC: The *Directory* is continually insistent that catechesis be specifically aimed at the life situation of those being evangelized: "The evangelization of the world finds itself placed in a very diversified and changing religious panorama, in which it is possible to distinguish three basic situations requiring particular and precise responses" (58). It then lists non-Christian cultures in which Christ is not known at all, and nominally Christian cultures where all sense of faith has been lost. Parts III and IV of the GDC give practical guidelines for adapting catechesis. Like Ignatius the GDC is attentive to the need to adapt to the needs of the individual.

Kingdom-Centered: Apostolic

IS: The central meditation of the Exercises is the meditation on Christ the King; Christ calls his disciples to follow him in all circumstances to win the world for his Father. "My will is to conquer the whole world and all my enemies, and thus to enter into the glory of my Father. Therefore, whoever wishes to come with me must labor with me, so that through following me in the pain he or she may follow me also in the glory." Ignatian spirituality is an active apostolic spirituality intended for those living in the midst of world events and activities.

GDC: Mission and kingdom are central: "Jesus declares that the Kingdom of God is inaugurated in him, in his very person. . . . Jesus shows, equally, that the community of his disciples, the Church, is, on earth, the seed and the beginning of that Kingdom and, like leaven in the dough, what she desires is that the Kingdom of God grow in the world like a great tree" (102). The *GDC* assumes that all will be active in spreading the Kingdom of God in their own particular circumstances.

Church-Centered

IS: Ignatius was a loyal churchman. In establishing the Society of Jesus he wished it to be an instrument for reform of the Church and for service to the Church wherever most needed; indeed most Jesuits take a fourth vow to serve the Church wherever the pope commands. Ignatius also included "Rules for Thinking with the Church" in the *Spiritual Exercises*.

GDC: The *Directory* is a Vatican document, approved by the Holy See, specifying that its teaching of the content of faith be in accord with the official *Catechism of the Catholic Church*: "Catechesis is essentially an ecclesial act. The true subject of catechesis is the Church which, continuing the mission of Jesus the Master, and therefore animated by the Holy Spirit, is sent to be the teacher of the faith." The genius of the *Directory* is that it combines good pedagogical principles with the teaching of faith contained in Scripture, Tradition, and teaching of the Magisterium.

Service of Faith and Promotion of Justice

IS: General Congregations 32, 33, and 34 have been in accord, orienting Jesuits today toward promotion of justice in the world, especially in situations of oppression: GC 32, *Our Mission Today*, 1975: "The mission of the Society of Jesus today is the service of faith, of which the promotion of justice is an absolute requirement." The Society has been responding to the call of the Second Vatican Council, especially *Gaudium et Spes*, and to recent Church documents (*Synod of Latin American Bishops in Medellin*, 1968) that all our ministries have a "preferential option for the poor."

GDC: The *Directory* echoes Church documents urging a special concern with the liberation of the oppressed: "The Good News of the Kingdom of God, which proclaims salvation, includes a message of liberation. . . . The Beatitudes of Jesus, addressed to those who suffer, are an eschatological proclamation of the salvation which the Kingdom brings. . . . The community of the disciples of Jesus, the Church, shares today the same sensitivity as the Master himself showed them. With great sorrow she turns her attention to those peoples who, as we all know, are striving with all their power and energy to overcome all those circumstances which compel them to live on the borderline of existence: hunger, chronic epidemics, illiteracy, poverty, injustice between nations (103)."

Principle of Realism: Discernment of Spirits

IS: Ignatius was aware that not every inner experience could be trusted. Consequently he presented guidelines for distinguishing inner experiences that were from God from those that were not from God, or in other words, those from the good spirit (Holy Spirit) and those from the evil spirit (Satan). He also encouraged a daily review of our activities to acknowledge our response to God's presence in them and to be realistic in acknowledging our possible sinfulness, that is, our lack of response to this presence.

GDC: This theme of Ignatian spirituality is not as present in the *GDC* as it is in the previous six examples. But the document does talk about metanoia and continuing conversion; on this level it is compatible with Ignatian spirituality: "Faith involves a change of life, a metanoia, that is a profound transformation of mind and heart; it causes the believer to live that conversion" (55); "Faith is a gift destined to grow in the hearts of believers. Adhering to Jesus Christ, in fact, sets in motion a process of continuing conversion, which lasts for the whole of life" (56).

Finding God and the Goals of Evangelization from Go and Make Disciples

In *Go Make Disciples: A National Plan and Strategy for Evangelization in the United States* the bishops of the United States outlined goals, obejectives, and strategies for proclaiming the gospel message and inviting Catholics to join in the mission of evangelization. *Finding God: Our Response to God's Gifts* implements the strategies that the bishops call for.

Goal 1: "To bring about in all Catholics such an enthusiasm for their faith that, in living their faith in Jesus, they freely share it with others"

Finding God: Our Response to God's Gifts creates an enthusiasm for the faith among catechists, children, and their parents and families by

~ CALLING THEM TO RENEWAL—The Catechist Guide speaks to catechists about their vocation and provides resources to deepen and renew their faith in order to better share it with children. The design of the children's book itself is inviting, enabling children to be enthusiastic about their faith because of the quality of the resource they will use. Parents and families are invited to renew their faith through use of the "Raising Faith-Filled Kids" pages, the Parent Newsletters, the Parents' Guide to Prayer, and the Gathering Sessions.

~ FOSTERING A GREATER APPRECIATION FOR GOD'S WORD IN THEIR LIVES—Scripture serves as a foundation for the content of each session, and the children's book includes at least two Scripture passages for each session. The catechist guide provides explanations to help the catechist develop a deeper understanding of the Scripture passages being used. The importance of the prayer center with an enthroned Bible highlights the role of God's Word.

~ HIGHLIGHTING THE CONNECTION BETWEEN EVANGELIZATION AND WORSHIP—The Link to Liturgy features provide solid connections between the sharing of our faith and our Catholic life of worship as known through liturgy and the sacraments.

~ INSTILLING A DEEPER LIFE OF PRAYER—The unique role of prayer in *Finding God: Our Response to God's Gifts* invites both catechists and children to a deeper prayer life. The three-minute retreat included in the catechist preparation section of the Catechist Guide encourages catechists to deepen their own prayers. Gathering Sessions include reflective prayer experiences to deepen the prayer life of all the adults of the parish.

~ CREATING A DEEPER SENSE OF THE HOME AS DOMESTIC CHURCH—*Finding God: Our Response to God's Gifts* teaches the importance of the domestic church and reinforces it throughout by including a "With My Family" feature in every session. Parents are supported in their efforts to build the domestic church through the use of the "Raising Faith-Filled Kids" pages, the Parent Newsletters, the Parents Guide to Prayer, and the Gathering Sessions.

~ FOSTERING A GREATER APPRECIATION OF CULTURAL AND SPIRITUAL DIVERSITY—The children's book reflects a deep understanding of the Church's cultural and spiritual diversity through stories, brief biographies of the lives of saints and holy people, fine art, photographs, and illustrations. The Catechist Guide treats the concept of cultural and spiritual diversity as an integral part of what it means to understand the catholicity of the Church.

Goal 2: "To invite all people, whatever their social or cultural background, to hear the message of salvation in Jesus Christ so they may come to join us in the fullness of the Catholic faith."

Finding God: Our Response to God's Gifts invites catechists, children, and their parents and families to hear the message of salvation in Jesus Christ by

~ CREATING A WELCOMING ATMOSPHERE THROUGHOUT THE PROGRAM—The Catechist Guide provides suggestions in each session for warmly welcoming the children and sending them off. With its beautiful art and intelligent design the children's book is a welcoming resource for children to use The catechetical leader is provided with opportunities to welcome parents and families through use of the "Raising Faith-Filled Kids" pages, the Parent Newsletters, and the Gathering Sessions.

~ INVITING THEM TO FEEL COMFORTABLE SHARING THEIR FAITH—Gathering Sessions for adults provide parents with an environment that is conducive for adult faith sharing, while the Parent Newsletters and "Raising Faith-Filled Kids" resources provide them with a deeper understanding of their faith so that they can be more comfortable sharing it with others. The Catechist Guide provides such depth of information for catechists that they will feel comfortable sharing their faith not only with the children but also with everyone they meet. The children's book provides clear explanations of the faith so that children will be more comfortable sharing their faith with others.

~ ENCOURAGING THE SHARING OF THE GOSPEL IN FAMILIES—"With My Family" features along with the "Raising Faith-Filled Kids" pages, the Parent Newsletters, and the Gathering Sessions encourage the sharing of the gospel in the home.

~ USING SPECIAL FAMILY TIMES TO INVITE PEOPLE TO FAITH—"With My Family" features along with the "Raising Faith-Filled Kids" pages, the Parent Newsletters, and the Gathering Sessions invite all parishioners and family members to faith.

Goal 3: "To foster gospel values in our society, promoting the dignity of the human person, the importance of the family, and the common good of our society, so that our nation may be transformed"

Finding God: Our Response to God's Gifts fosters gospel values among catechists, children, and their parents and families that promote the dignity of the human person, the importance of the family, and the common good of our society by

~ ADDRESSING THE NEEDS OF PEOPLE IN THEIR AREAS—The Respond feature of every session encourages children to identify, with the help of the catechist and catechetical leader, realistic ways of addressing the needs of people in their community and around the world. The catechist is provided with numerous other optional activities that help to address children's needs. The "With My Family" feature encourages children to work with their family to be of service to others and to address the needs of others. Catholic Social Teaching throughout the program highlights the need for Catholics to serve the Kingdom of God by building a just society and living a life of holiness. Activities throughout the program invite children to work with their catechists and families to be aware of the ways our nation and world might be transformed by Jesus and, to the extent that transformation is possible, ways in which they, themselves, might work to support those changes.

~ FOSTERING THE IMPORTANCE OF THE FAMILY—*Finding God: Our Response to God's Gifts* highlights the importance of the family and reinforces it throughout by including a "With My Family" feature in every session. Parents are supported in their efforts to build the domestic church through the use of the "Raising Faith-Filled Kids" pages, the Parent Newsletters, the Parent Guide to Prayer, and the Gathering Sessions.

~ EXPLORING ISSUES OF THE WORKPLACE AND LAY SPIRITUALITY—The universal call to holiness is highlighted in the program as is the notion of vocation and understanding God's call to serve the Kingdom in whatever capacity we are capable. Catholic Social teaching throughout the program emphasizes the dignity of work and the rights of workers.

NOTES

1. Matthias Neumann, O.S.B., *Christology: True God, True Man* (Chicago: Loyola Press, 2002), p. 83.

2. Kevin Hughes, *Church History: Faith Handed On* (Chicago: Loyola Press, 2002), p. 23.

3. Ibid., p. 41.

4. "Catechesis, II (Medieval)," in *New Catholic Encyclopedia* 2nd ed., vol. 3 (Washington, D.C.: The Catholic University of America, 2002), p. 230.

5. Hughes, *Church History,* pp. 57–58.

6. Neumann, *Christology*, p. 48.

7. "General Catechetical Directory," in Archdiocese of Chicago, *The Catechetical Documents: A Parish Resource* (Chicago: Liturgy Training Publications, 1996), 11.

8. "To Teach As Jesus Did: A Pastoral Message on Catholic Education," in Archdiocese of Chicago, *The Catechetical Documents: A Parish Resource* (Chicago: Liturgy Training Publications, 1996) 19.

9. Ibid. 23.

10. Ibid. 27.

11. Ibid. 43.

12. "Basic Teachings for Catholic Religious Education," in Archdiocese of Chicago, *The Catechetical Documents: A Parish Resource* (Chicago: Liturgy Training Publications, 1996), introduction.

13. Ibid.

14. "Basic Teachings," introduction to theme 3.

15. "On Evangelization in the Modern World," in Archdiocese of Chicago, *The Catechetical Documents: A Parish Resource* (Chicago: Liturgy Training Publications, 1996) 14.

16. "Sharing the Light of Faith: National Catechetical Directory," in Archdiocese of Chicago, *The Catechetical Documents: A Parish Resource* (Chicago: Liturgy Training Publications, 1996) 32.

17. NCD 170.

18. "On Catechesis in Our Time." In Archdiocese of Chicago, *The Catechetical Documents: A Parish Resource* (Chicago: Liturgy Training Publications, 1996) 26.

19. CT 13.

20. CT 15.

21. Giles Cusson, S.J., *Biblical Theology and the Spiritual Exercises* (St. Louis: Institute of Jesuit Resources, 1994), p. 63.

22. Monica Hellwig, *Finding God in All Things: A Spirituality for Today* (Ignatian Apostolic Partnership, 2001). http://www.ignatianpartners.org/hellwig.htm.

23. David Lonsdale, *Eyes to See, Ears to Hear: An Introduction to Ignatian Spirituality.* (Maryknoll, N.Y.: Orbis Books, 2000), p. 22.

24. Philip Caramann, *Ignatius Loyola: A Biography of the Founder of the Jesuits* (San Francisco: Harper and Row, 1990), pp. 59–60.

25. Joseph A. Munit and Philip Endrean, trans. *Saint Ignatius of Loyola: Personal Writings* (London: Penguin Books, 1996), p. 56.

26. "The Vision Statement of the Society of Jesus." *Exposcit Debitum.* Approved by Pope Julius III and inserted in the Bull, 1550. http://jesuits.org.za.mission.htm.

27. William J. Young, S.J., *Letters of St. Ignatius of Loyola.* (Chicago: Loyola University Press, 1959), p. 95.

28. Ibid, pp. 95–96.

29. John O'Malley, S.J., "Early Jesuit Spirituality: Spain and Italy," in *Christian Spirituality: Post Reformation and Modern,* ed. Louis Dupre and Don E. Sailers (New York: Crossroad, 1991), p. 25.

30. John O'Malley, S.J., *The First Jesuits* (Cambridge: Harvard University Press, 1993), pp. 121–122).

31. "Guidelines for Doctrinally Sound Catechetical Materials," in *Archdiocese of Chicago, The Catechetical Documents: A Parish Resource* (Chicago: Liturgy Training Publications, 1996) 32.

32. CT 27.

ABBREVIATIONS

BT   Basic Teachings for Catholic Religious Education

CCC   *Catechism of the Catholic Church*

CT   On Catechesis in Our Time

EN   On Evangelization in the Modern World

GCD   General Catechetical Directory

GDC   *General Directory for Catechesis*

NCD   National Catechetical Directory: Sharing the Light of Faith

TJD   To Teach As Jesus Did